UNDER THE
microscope

VIRUSES
IN OUR WORLD

WRITTEN BY JOHN WOOD

I'M VICKY THE VIRUS, AND THIS IS CELLFRED, MY BUTLER. WE'LL BE YOUR GUIDES IN YOUR JOURNEY UNDER THE MICROSCOPE!

Cellfred

Vicky

KidHaven
PUBLISHING

MAR 1 0 2020

Published in 2020 by
**KidHaven Publishing, an Imprint of
Greenhaven Publishing, LLC**
353 3rd Avenue
Suite 255
New York, NY 10010

© 2020 Booklife Publishing

This edition is published by arrangement with Booklife
Publishing

Edited by: Kirsty Holmes
Designed by: Amy Li

Cataloging-in-Publication Data

Names: Wood, John.
Title: Viruses in our world / John Wood.
Description: New York : KidHaven Publishing, 2020. | Series:
Under the microscope | Includes glossary and index.
Identifiers: ISBN 9781534533257 (pbk.) | ISBN 9781534533271
(library bound) | ISBN 9781534533264 (6 pack) | ISBN
9781534533288 (ebook)
Subjects: LCSH: Viruses--Juvenile literature.
Classification: LCC QR365.W663 2020 | DDC 579.2--dc23

Printed in the United States of America

CPSIA compliance information: Batch #BW20KL: For further information contact
Greenhaven Publishing LLC, New York, New York at 1-844-317-7404.

Please visit our website, www.greenhavenpublishing.com. For
a free color catalog of all our high-quality books, call toll free
1-844-317-7404 or fax 1-844-317-7405.

PHOTO CREDITS

All images courtesy of Shutterstock. With thanks to Getty Images, Thinkstock Photo, and iStockphoto.

Front Cover – Carlos E. Santa Maria, givaga, ananaline, Kateryna Kon, nechaevkon, Somboon Bunpray,
espies, Supaleka_P, Master Images – ananaline (Cellfred), givaga, FabrikaSimf (title and label masking tape),
andy0man (paper texture), science_photo (petri dish borders) 1 – Carlos E. Santa Maria,
4 – Rawpixel.com, 5 – BlurryMe, 6 – Nenad Zivkovic, 7 – Elizaveta Galitckaia, 8 – Zurijeta, Oleksandr
Khokhlyuk, 10 – NIAID (wikipedia), 11 – Everett Hospital (wikipedia), 12 – konstantinks, 13 – Chaikom, 14 –
jaddingt, 15 – AuntSpray, 16 – Suzanne Tucker, 17 – connel, 18 – AuntSpray, 19 – Kateryna Kon,
20 – hanapon1002, 21 – Africa Studio, 22 – Phonlamai Photo, toeytoey, 23 – Konsan Loonprom.

CONTENTS

WORDS THAT LOOK LIKE THIS CAN BE FOUND IN THE GLOSSARY ON PAGE 24.

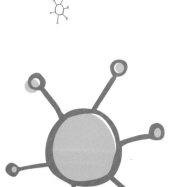

WHAT ARE VIRUSES?

Viruses are tiny **organisms** that make people sick. Viruses make their home in cells. Cells are like the building blocks of life.

ANIMALS, PLANTS, AND EVEN PEOPLE ARE MADE UP OF LOTS OF CELLS JOINED TOGETHER.

Viruses are very simple organisms. In fact, they are so simple that nobody is sure whether they are alive or not!

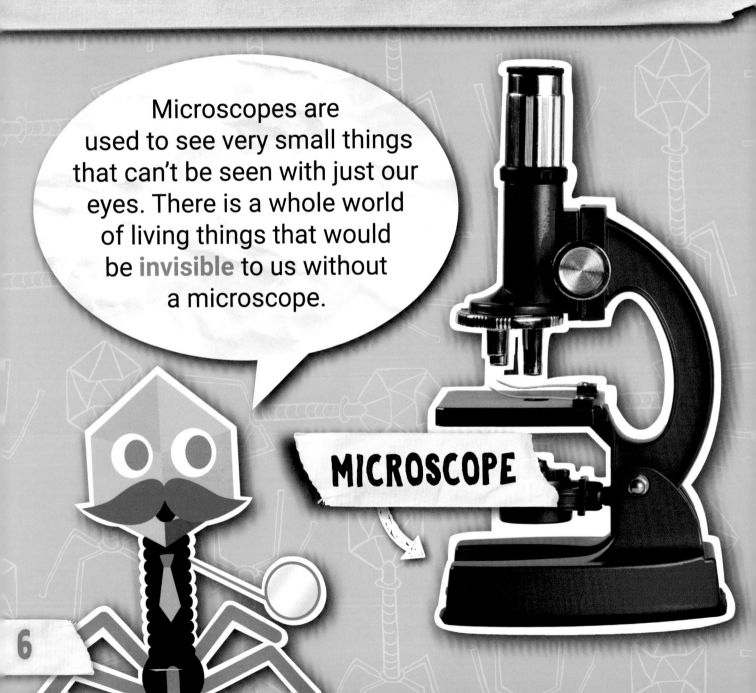

Microscopes are used to see very small things that can't be seen with just our eyes. There is a whole world of living things that would be **invisible** to us without a microscope.

MICROSCOPE

6

Some microscopes are more powerful than others. Scientists use very powerful microscopes, like the one in the picture below.

MOST VIRUSES ARE SO SMALL THAT THEY CAN'T EVEN BE SEEN THROUGH NORMAL MICROSCOPES.

IT IS TIME TO EXPLORE THE TINY WORLD OF VIRUSES. LET'S GO MEET SOME!

7

INFLUENZA

Influenza – known as the flu – is a virus that can make someone very sick. They might cough and vomit, or have a sore throat. They might also have diarrhea (say: die-ah-ree-ah), which means runny poop!

FLU CAN CAUSE A FEVER. THIS MAKES A PERSON FEEL VERY HOT.

The flu virus travels mainly by sneezing, coughing, and talking. Droplets from the **infected** person are breathed in by other people, spreading the virus.

FLU FROM OTHER ANIMALS, SUCH AS BIRDS AND PIGS, CAN ALSO INFECT PEOPLE.

LET'S TURN THE PAGE AND LOOK UNDER THE MICROSCOPE!

All living things make more of themselves. Animals have babies, while plants make seeds. Even **bacteria**, which are each made up of one cell, split in two.

THIS IS SWINE FLU, A TYPE OF FLU VIRUS THAT COMES FROM PIGS.

SWINE FLU VIRUS

Viruses trick cells into helping them create more copies of the virus. Soon the cell bursts, and the copies go to find other cells to infect.

VIRUSES CAN
ONLY MAKE MORE
OF THEMSELVES WHEN
THEY INVADE
A CELL.

EBOLA

Some viruses are more dangerous than others. Ebola is a type of deadly virus. Luckily it is quite rare in most parts of the world.

AFRICA

CÔTE D'IVOIRE

SUDAN

GABON

UGANDA

DEMOCRATIC REPUBLIC OF THE CONGO

EBOLA WAS FIRST FOUND IN AFRICA. THE YELLOW PARTS OF THIS MAP SHOW INFECTED AREAS.

Unlike the flu, Ebola doesn't spread through the air – it spreads through touch. If the virus enters the body, such as through the mouth or a cut, the person becomes infected.

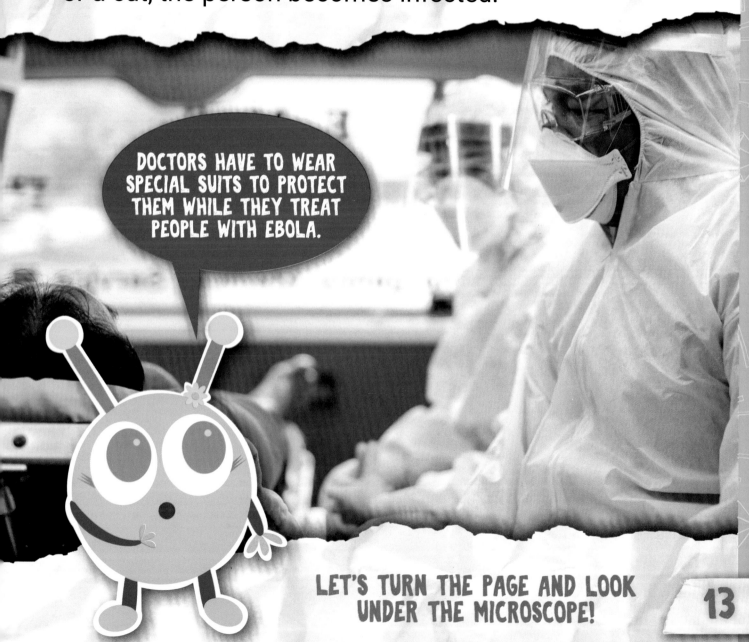

DOCTORS HAVE TO WEAR SPECIAL SUITS TO PROTECT THEM WHILE THEY TREAT PEOPLE WITH EBOLA.

LET'S TURN THE PAGE AND LOOK UNDER THE MICROSCOPE!

The body has a sort of alarm that tells it a virus is present and needs to be beaten. However, Ebola is dangerous because it doesn't set the alarm off.

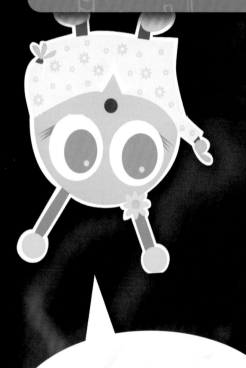

THE EBOLA VIRUS CAN LIVE ON DRY SURFACES, OR IN BODILY FLUIDS.

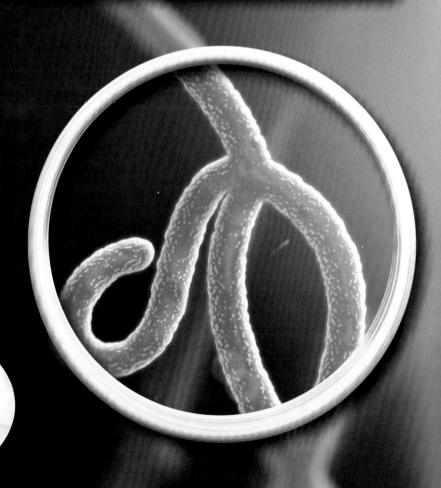

The body attacks the cells infected with Ebola. However, the attack is so powerful that it often damages the **blood vessels**, which can be fatal.

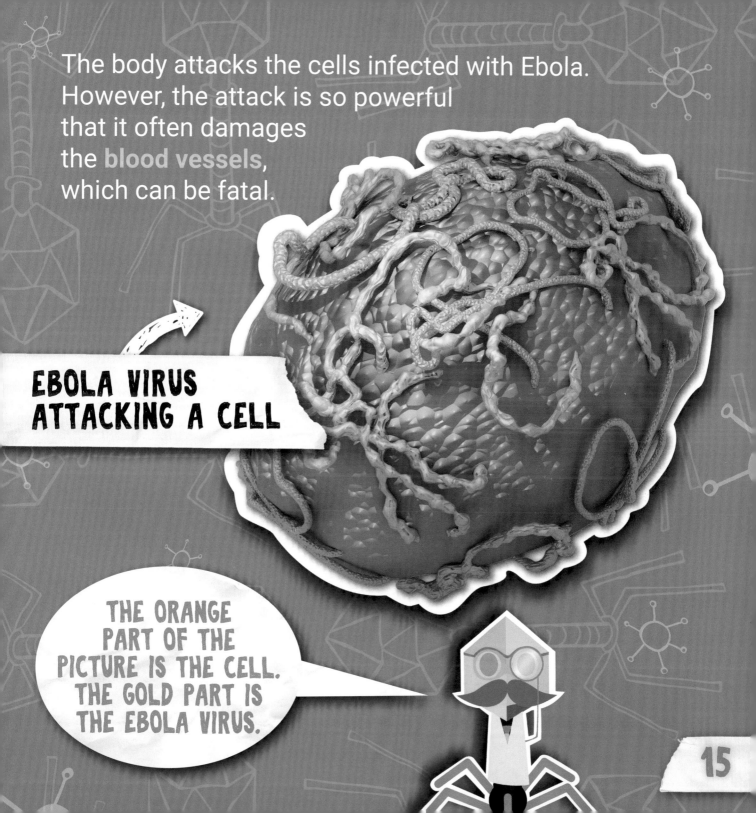

EBOLA VIRUS ATTACKING A CELL

THE ORANGE PART OF THE PICTURE IS THE CELL. THE GOLD PART IS THE EBOLA VIRUS.

GOOD VIRUSES

Not all viruses go after animals and humans. Some of them infect bad types of bacteria that can be harmful to other living things. A virus that goes after bacteria is called a bacteriophage (say: bac-teer-ee-ah-fayge).

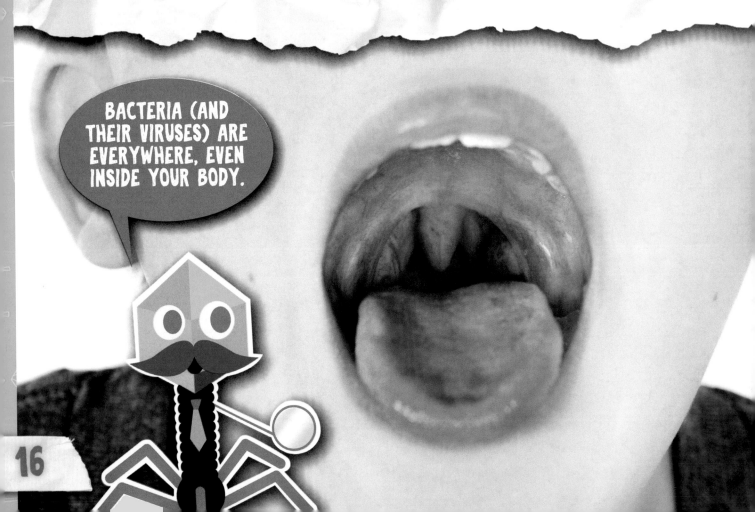

BACTERIA (AND THEIR VIRUSES) ARE EVERYWHERE, EVEN INSIDE YOUR BODY.

There are more bacteriophages than any other virus in the world. They are found wherever bacteria are found, from the soil to the ocean.

BACTERIA ARE ON YOUR BODY, IN YOUR SCHOOL, AND EVEN ON THIS BOOK!

LET'S TURN THE PAGE AND LOOK UNDER THE MICROSCOPE!

Many bacteriophages have tails with little fibers on the end. The tail joins on to a bacteria cell. The virus then injects a part of itself inside the cell.

MANY VIRUSES ARE AROUND 1,000 TIMES SMALLER THAN MOST TYPES OF BACTERIA.

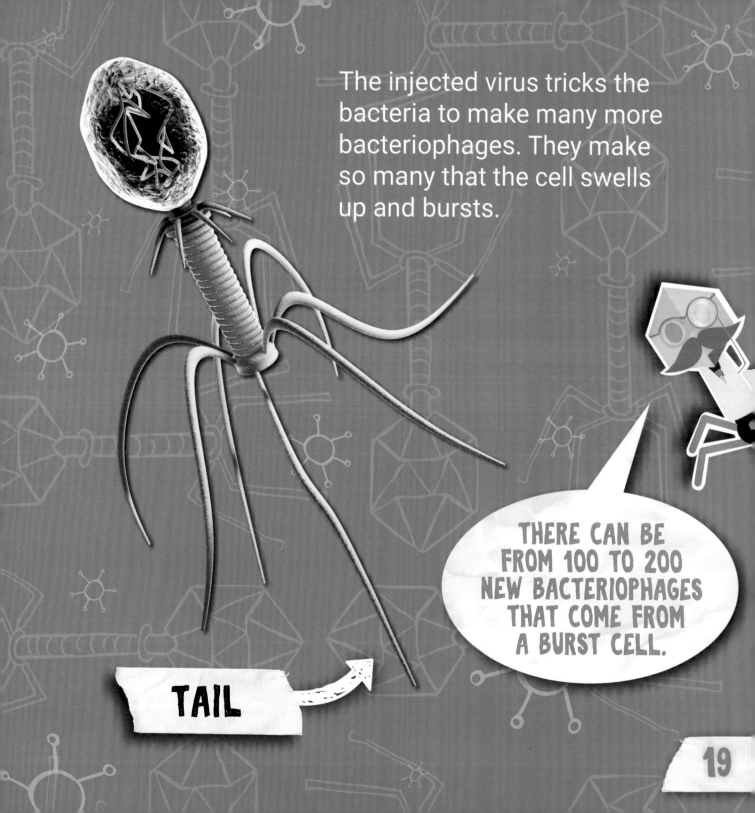

The injected virus tricks the bacteria to make many more bacteriophages. They make so many that the cell swells up and bursts.

THERE CAN BE FROM 100 TO 200 NEW BACTERIOPHAGES THAT COME FROM A BURST CELL.

TAIL

VACCINES

Viruses can be hard to cure because they hide in our cells. Mostly we have to let our bodies deal with them. But there is a way to help our bodies.

WASHING OUR HANDS CAN CLEAN AWAY VIRUSES BEFORE THEY INFECT THE BODY.

A vaccine is an injection of a weak form of a disease. Your body learns how to fight the weak disease, and other deadlier diseases just like it.

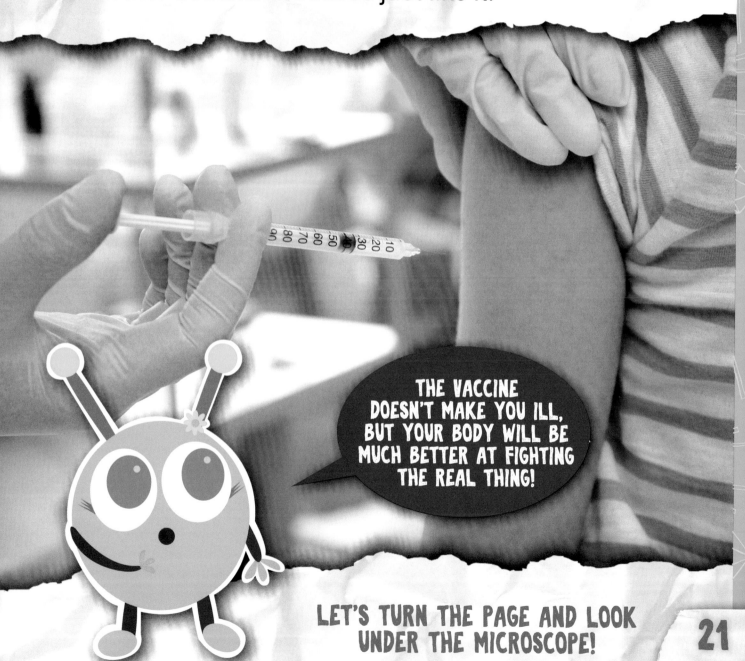

THE VACCINE DOESN'T MAKE YOU ILL, BUT YOUR BODY WILL BE MUCH BETTER AT FIGHTING THE REAL THING!

LET'S TURN THE PAGE AND LOOK UNDER THE MICROSCOPE!

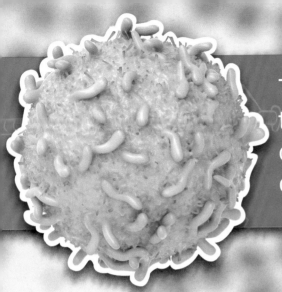

The body creates white blood cells to destroy a virus. Some white blood cells gobble up viruses, while others create **antibodies** that kill viruses.

THERE ARE MANY TYPES OF WHITE BLOOD CELLS LIKE THIS THAT WORK TOGETHER TO KEEP YOU SAFE.

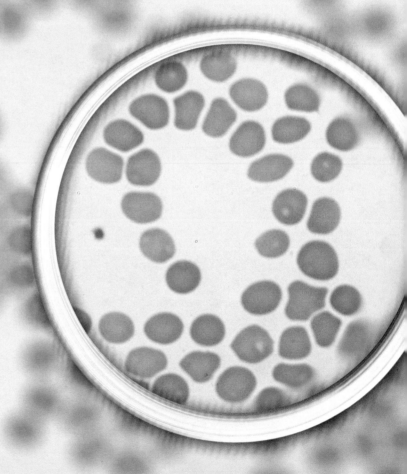